Paul Durcan was born in Dublin in 1944, of County Mayo parents. He studied archaeology and medieval history at University College Cork. In 1974 he won the Patrick Kavanagh Award and he received Creative Writing Bursaries from The Arts Council/An Chomhairle Ealaíon, Ireland, in 1976 and 1980. He has given readings of his poems throughout the world. In 1981 he represented Ireland at the Struga Poetry Festival in Yugoslavia and in 1983 undertook a tour of the Soviet Union at the invitation of the Union of Soviet Writers. In May 1985 he was resident poet at The Frost Place, New Hampshire. He revisited the Soviet Union in autumn 1986. In February 1987 he gave readings in Saskatoon and Toronto, and in June 1987 he represented Ireland at the Poetry International in Rotterdam. In March 1988 he gave readings in Montreal, New Brunswick and Nova Scotia, and in April 1988 he undertook a tour of Italy. In June 1988 he read at the South Bank Festival of Poetry. He is a member of Aosdána.

Among Paul Durcan's published works are:

Endsville (with Brian Lynch), New Writers Press, Dublin, 1967

O Westport in the Light of Asia Minor, Anna Livia Press, Dublin, 1975

Teresa's Bar, Gallery Press, Dublin, 1976, 1986

Sam's Cross, Profile Press, Dublin, 1978

Jesus, Break His Fall, Raven Arts Press, Dublin, 1980

Ark of the North, Raven Arts Press, Dublin, 1982

The Selected Paul Durcan, Blackstaff Press, Belfast, 1982 (Poetry Ireland Choice), 1985

Jumping the Train Tracks with Angela, Raven Arts Press, Dublin/Carcanet New Press, Manchester, 1983

The Berlin Wall Café, Blackstaff Press, Belfast, 1985 (Poetry Book Society Choice)

Going Home to Russia, Blackstaff Press, Belfast, 1987

Jesus and Angela

Jesus and Angela
poems

PAUL DURCAN

THE
BLACKSTAFF
PRESS
BELFAST AND ST PAUL, MINNESOTA

First published in 1988 by
The Blackstaff Press Limited
3 Galway Park, Dundonald, Belfast BT16 0AN, Northern Ireland
and
Box 5026, 2115 Summit Avenue, St Paul, Minnesota 55105, USA
with the assistance of
The Arts Council of Northern Ireland

Printed by The Guernsey Press Company Limited

British Library Cataloguing in Publication Data
Durcan, Paul, 1944–
Jesus and Angela.
1. Title
821'.914

Library of Congress Cataloging-in-Publication Data
Durcan, Paul, 1944–
Jesus and Angela / Paul Durcan.
p.   cm.
Selections from: Jesus, break his fall and Jumping the train
tracks with Angela.
1. Durcan, Paul, 1944–. Jesus, break his fall. Selections.
1988. II. Durcan, Paul, 1944–. Jumping the train tracks with
Angela. Selections. 1988. III. Title.
PR6054.U72J47   1988   88–7430
821'.914—dc19   CIP

ISBN 0-85640-407-1

to
DERMOT BOLGER

. . . the mind of man is on the whole less tortuous
when he is love-making than at any other time. . .
[it is when he] speaks of governments and armies
that he utters strange and dangerous nonsense
to please the bats at the back of his soul.
Rebecca West

ACKNOWLEDGEMENTS

This book is the author's selection (with revisions) from work originally published in two separate books: *Jesus, Break His Fall*, Raven Arts Press, 1980, and *Jumping the Train Tracks with Angela*, Raven Arts Press/Carcanet New Press, 1983.

CONTENTS

PART I

The Drimoleague Blues   3
Sally   4
Granny Tree in the Sky   5
That Propeller I Left in Bilbao   6
Save Eden Quay   8
Mr Goldsmith, My Father's Friend   10
The Daughter Finds Her Father Dead   12
Mary Carey in Paris, June 1979   14
Hopping Round Knock Shrine in the Falling
    Rain: 1958   15
The Man Whose Name Was Tom-and-Ann   16
Little Old Ladies Also Can Write Poems such as
    This Poem Written in Widow's Blood in a Rented
    Top-Storey Room in Downtown Cork   17
Tullynoe: Tête-à-Tête in the Parish Priest's Parlour   19
Charlie's Mother   20
Spitting the Pips Out – with the College Lecturer in
    Philosophy   22
KK's Lament for GG   24
The Bearded Nun   25
The Anatomy of Divorce by Joe Commonwealth   26
My Twenty-Seven Psychiatrists   27
En Famille, 1979   27
Madman   27
Maimie   28
Marriage, Deafness, and the Problem of Erosion   28
Naked Girl in Boardroom of Financiers,
    South Mall, Cork   28
Honeymoon Postcard   29
This Week the Court Is Sleeping in Loughrea   30
Bartle and Lulu: Channel Zero   31
Munch   32
Veronica Shee from the Town of Tralee   33

On Seeing Two Bus Conductors Kissing Each Other
   in the Middle of the Street   34
The Boy Who Was Conceived in the Leithreas   35
A Funk in Obelisk   37
For My Lord Tennyson I Shall Lay Down My Life   39
The Death by Heroin of Sid Vicious   40

PART II

The Crucifixion Circus, Good Friday, Paris 1981   43

PART III

The Man Whose Name Was Shakespeare   49
The Woman Who Keeps Her Breasts in the Back Garden   50
Watching Michael Cullen's Strawberry Nude with Friend   51
The Rose of Blackpool   53
The Problem of Fornication on the Blarney Chronicle   55
Old Lady, Middle Parish   57
Michelangelo Road   59
Our Lady of the Black Tree, Paris 1981   60
The Perfect Nazi Family Is Alive and Well and Prospering
   in Modern Ireland   62
Interview for a Job   64
The Child on the Train, Yorkshire 1980   66
Rory Carty and Son: High-Class Butchers   67
The Night They Put John Lennon Down   68
Papua, New Guinea   70
The Harpist   71
Vincent Crane – the Enniskerry Brat   72
Mother's Blues   73
The Elephant House in Berlin Zoo   75

PART IV

Jumping the Train Tracks with Angela   79
The Children of Hiroshima, Dublin 7   81
The Last Bus to Ballyfermot   84

Forty-Eight Hours in Bed with Joanna   86
World Cup '82   88
Brother, Can You Spare a Valium?   89
Dave Loves Macker 14.2.83   91
Blind Young Man, Virginia   92
Trinity College Dublin, 1983   94
The Lion Tamer   95
The Golden Girl   96
Going Home to Meet Sylvia   98

PART
I

The Drimoleague Blues

for Sarah and Síabhra

Oh I know this mean town is not always mean
And I know that you do not always mean what you mean
And the meaning of meaning can both mean and not mean:
But I mean to say, I mean to say,
I've got the Drimoleague Blues, I've got the Drimoleague Blues,
I've got the Drimoleague Blues so bad I can't move:
Even if you were to plug in Drimoleague to every oil well in
    Arabia –
I'd still have the Drimoleague Blues.

Oh this town is so mean that it's got its own mean
And that's to be as mean as green, as mean as green:
Shoot a girl dead and win yourself a bride,
Shoot a horse dead and win yourself a car.
Oh I've got the Drimoleague Blues, I've got the Drimoleague
    Blues,
I've got the Drimoleague Blues so bad I can't move:
Even if you were to plug in Drimoleague to every oil well in
    Arabia –
I'd still have the Drimoleague Blues.

And so on right down to the end of the line
Mean with Mean will always rhyme
And Man with Man: O where is the Woman
With the Plough, where is her Daughter with the Stars?
Oh I've got the Drimoleague Blues, I've got the Drimoleague
    Blues,
I've got the Drimoleague Blues so bad I can't move:
Even if you were to plug in Drimoleague to every oil well in
    Arabia –
I'd still have the Drimoleague Blues.

Sally

Sally, I was happy with *you*.

Yet a dirty cafeteria in a railway station –
In the hour before dawn over a formica table
Confettied with cigarette ash and coffee stains –
Was all we ever knew of a home together.

'Give me a child and let me go':
'Give me a child and let me stay':
She to him and he to her:
Which said *which* and *who* was *who*?

Sally, I was happy with *you*.

Granny Tree in the Sky

Grandmother is all bleak and bare
While the alien whom I do not know
Fattens golden on the cliff edge.

Yet although our bones rot more rotten than we know
Or than we care to know,
Although we find God's cushion but not God,

And although we are all in our blue-black way
Bleaker and barer than you are,
And we cannot be comic in Dachau,

Dear skeleton, all bleak and bare,
Dear agèd tree, heaped in dissolution,
You are yet beanstalk to us all,

Toothless in Tír na nÓg.
Beanstalk to us all. Beanstalk to us all.

That Propeller I Left in Bilbao

Would you like a whiskey? Good.
That's my girl: how I do like to see
You with a glass of whiskey in your hand,
And that gleam of a smile beneath your hat:

And that gleam of a smile beneath your hat:
But that propeller I left in Bilbao –
I ought to tell you about it now –
But blast it, I won't: let's have a row:

Ow: ow: ow: let's have a row:
Let's pink the pink floor pinker than pink:
I am a pink place in which a pink pig plashes:
You are a pink peach in which a pink babe perishes –

Perishes to be born! Put in a new cassette!
And let the cherry-blossom blossom till it fall
Asunder – O my Pink Thunder – asunder
And that propeller I left in Bilbao

Is still that propeller I left in Bilbao:
But you have sheared off all your robes
And you would like, if it pleases me, a second whiskey:
Why of course, my Big Pink Thunderbird –

My Big Pink Thunderbird – why of course –
Do you know how many telephone calls I had today?
The flaming phone never stopped flaming ringing
And all about that propeller I left in Bilbao:

All about that propeller I left in Bilbao:
I said: 'Telex' to them all: 'Telex':
And now to you, love, Telex For Ever and For Ever Telex,
And may that propeller I left in Bilbao,

Well – may that propeller I left in Bilbao –
That propeller I left in Bilbao –
Propeller I left in Bilbao –
I left in Bilbao.

Save Eden Quay

Indeed save Wood Quay:
But what about *me*?
My name is Eden Quay:
Please save *me*.

Oh all these lorries
— Articulated how-are-yis —
Have me strangled nearly:
Save me, save Eden Quay.

Many is the he-and-she
Who queued up on top of me
To get a seat in the Corinthian
Or to get a 7A home.

Many is the he-and-she
Or she-and-she, or he, or she,
Queued up for the new movie
Being projected in three-D:

Vincent Price — so ugly
And suave, and smugly
Sawing up women:
Grimacing, grinning.

Or next door in the Astor,
Motoring faster and faster
In France, a screw in the roadster
Getting looser and looser.

Or Antonioni —
A black-and-white map of the agony
Of human love, where night
Is day, and day is night.

You fucking architects
Think of nothing but sex:
Cities are not for living in,
They're only for fucking in.

But you won't wait a jiffy,
Will you? 'I'll kill you,'
You squeal at the Liffey:
You won't wait a jiffy.

And what about Burgh Quay
Across the river from *me*?
What about David Marcus?
Where all the lark is?

Indeed save Wood Quay:
But save also Burgh Quay:
My name is Eden Quay:
PLEASE SAVE ME.

1979

9

Mr Goldsmith, My Father's Friend

My father who was stern and staid
Had a most peculiar friend,
The uproarious Mr Goldsmith,
Who stammered so much at the hall door,
One night he fell flat on the floor,
And who did not use the upstairs toilet
But relieved himself in the garden.

My father indeed was a legal man
– Cut off, therefore, from the rest of man –
Except for Mr Goldsmith, who
Returned from London with a stolen
Police helmet for us children,
And who did not use the upstairs toilet
But relieved himself in the garden.

Yes, my father who was so saturnine
Had a most delightful friend,
The uproarious Mr Goldsmith,
Who laughed so much at supper time,
He spattered the tablecloth with wine,
And who did not use the upstairs toilet
But relieved himself in the garden.

But my father who was stern and staid
Cherished his most peculiar friend
For being verbally delirious,
When people said it was not right
That a grown-up man should talk all night,
And who did not use the upstairs toilet
But relieved himself in the garden.

My father, extremely vehemently,
Defended his most peculiar friend,
The uproarious Mr Goldsmith,

Who was expelled from boarding school
Because he broke the golden rule,
And who did not use the upstairs toilet
But relieved himself in the garden.

Perhaps my very serious father
Was the hand that helped to shove the arm
Of the needle when it stuck in the groove;
Shoved the wheel stuck in the rut
When Mr Goldsmith could not utt—
Who di-did not use the upstairs toi-toilet
But re-relieved himself in the ga-garden.

Oh Mr Goldsmith, Mr Goldsmith,
That you were a black man red as veal
Engulfed me but did not threaten.
I was at an age when books were real
And all the world was full of colour.
And I was proud of my father's friend,
Who did not use the upstairs toilet
But relieved himself in the garden.

The Daughter Finds Her Father Dead

for A.D.

The day that Father died
I went up to wake him at 8.30 a.m.
Before I left home for school:
The night before he had said
Before I went up to bed:
'Remember to wake me at 8.30 a.m.
Remember to wake me at 8.30 a.m.'

The day that Father died
At 8.30 a.m. I went up to wake him
And I thought at first he was dead:
He did not move when I shook him,
But then he said, then he said:
'Rider Haggard, Rider Haggard:
Storm Jameson, Storm Jameson.'

The day that Father died
Those were the last words he said:
'Rider Haggard, Rider Haggard:
Storm Jameson, Storm Jameson.'
I thought then he was alive
But he was dead, he was dead;
When I came from school he was dead.

The day that Father died
I glimpsed him telescopically:
Inside in his eyes inside in his head
A small voice in a faraway world
Spinning like a tiny coin:
'Rider Haggard, Rider Haggard:
Storm Jameson, Storm Jameson.'

Apparently – I suppose I should say
'It seems' – Father was a man

Who thought God was a woman
And that was why he was always sad,
Bad at being glad:
'Rider Haggard, Rider Haggard:
Storm Jameson, Storm Jameson.'

He cries and he cries, over and over,
In the empty nights that are emptier
And the dark days that are darker:
'Rider Haggard, Rider Haggard:
Storm Jameson, Storm Jameson':
And I take a look out from my bunk bed
As if all the world were a black silhouette

Or an infinite series of black silhouettes
Brokenly riding the white skyline:
'Rider Haggard, Rider Haggard:
Storm Jameson, Storm Jameson':
And just as my father thought God was a woman,
I think God is a man: are both of us wrong?
O if only a horse could write a song:

O if only a horse could write a song.

Mary Carey in Paris, June 1979

Pour me a new man – no milk, no sugar –
I am ready now for come what may.
Listen: the bird of suicide is poignantly silent
Although a zillion Citroëns zoom past to doom.

Pour me a new man – no milk, no sugar –
In our own time we will find out if we rhyme.
And if not – well, dissonance is music to my ears –
And besides, it was women who taught men how to swim.

Pour me a new man – no milk, no sugar –
I remember him in the far-off days of the future
Before he became famous and never smiled again.
Ah for a bit of fun and a kiss or two in a taxi!

Underneath the Awnings of Loneliness the sun glows
In all that passes as well as in all that stays.
O you who would stay with me, pass on, pass on.
Good night, Sir Fast; Good morning, Comrade Slow.

Pour me a new man – no milk, no sugar –
Who is not all Slug Her and Tug Her, Mug Her and Bug Her,
A man who can, and will, dance the cancan:
A man for a woman who knows how to man her.

Court me with the liqueurs of your eyes
And with the red wine of your mouth;
And with the brandy of your hands on my thighs
And with awkward truth, not with silken lies.

I drink to what I think: cognac, therefore I am.
To a stranger who never came
With his one foot in Budapest and his other in the Seine.
To a glass of man: O now pour me a new man.

Hopping Round Knock Shrine in the Falling Rain: 1958

to Karol Wojtyla

When I was thirteen I broke my leg.

Being the sensible, superstitious old lady that she was,
My Aunt Sarah knew that while to Know God was good,
To Get the Ear of his Mother was a more practical step:
Kneeling on the flagstone floor of her kitchen, all teaspoons
    and whins,
Outspoken as Moses, she called out Litanies to Our Lady:
The trick was to circumambulate the Shrine fifteen times
Repeating the rosary, telling your beads.
And so: that is how I came to be
Hopping round Knock Shrine in the Falling Rain.

In the Heel of that Spiritual Hunt
I became a Falling Figure clinging to the Shrine Wall
While Mayo rain pelleted down, jamming and jetting:
And while all the stalls – of relics, and phials of holy water,
And souvenir grottoes, and souvenir postcards,
And spheres which, when shaken, shook with fairy snow,
And sticks of Knock Rock –
Were being folded up for the day, I veered on,
Falling round Knock Shrine in the Hopping Rain.

Gable, O Gable, is there no Respite to thy Mercy?

The trick did not work
But that is scarcely the point:
That day was a crucial day
In my hedge school of belief,
In the Potential of Miracle,
In the Actuality of Vision:
And, therefore, I am grateful
For my plateful
Of Hopping round Knock Shrine in the Falling Rain.

The Man Whose Name Was Tom-and-Ann

When you enter a room where there is a party in progress
Normally you ignore the introductions:
This is Tom; and Jerry; and Micky; and Mouse –
They are all much the same – male mouths
Malevolent with magnanimity or females
Grinning gratuitously: but tonight
I paid attention when I was introduced to a man
Whose name was Tom-and-Ann:
All night I looked hard at him from all angles,
Even going so far as to look down his brass neck,
But all I could see was a young middle-aged man
With coal-black hair cut in a crew cut such
As would make you freeze, or faint, of electric shock:
Nobody had noticed that his wife was not with him:
She was at another party being introduced to *my* wife
Who, when she came home, started humming,
'Tonight I met a woman whose name was Ann-and-Tom.'

Well, next time I throw a party for all the Foleys in Ireland,
God help us, I will do the introductions myself:
'Darling Donal – this is Tom-and-Ann
And his beautiful wife Ann-and-Tom.'

Little Old Ladies Also Can Write Poems such as This Poem Written in Widow's Blood in a Rented Top-Storey Room in Downtown Cork

The light in the window went out last night.
For four years I had grown used to that light
In the window on the opposite side of the street.
All night, every night, for four total years

It glowed in the china-shop dark while I read
Autobiography after autobiography, waiting for daybreak.
Daybreak when at last I could shut
My eye flaps and grope my way

Into a coal cellar of half-sleep. The light
In the opposite window had a shredded saffron face.
But to whom it belonged I never knew.
That it glowed was enough, dedicatedly,

Punctually, courteously, over the innumerable,
Serrated, and always-darkening years.
'Kind saffron light' – I used chirp when I'd
Peer out my window at the window on the opposite

Side of the street. I'd say there are at least
Fifteen, maybe twenty, alive in that house,
Men and women, but because – in a manner of speaking –
I sleep by day – I never see these people.

Or if I do, it is only their overcoated spines that I see
As they teeter in the porch, foostering with key-rings.
In any case, they all wear hats and raincoats
And sometimes they have suitcases in their hands.

Light that was gold fruit in an amber tea towel
And I was a moth in the penumbra of its core;

No one swiped at me with yesterday's newspapers
Or slapped at my mouth with the soles of slippers.

This morning I did not go to sleep.
I waited for the coffin to come – and it did.
Two men carried it in and four men carried it out.
Such is the Weight of Light.

In the city cemetery now, under earth,
The Light of my Mind glows downward alone.
I can feel the transvestite worms massaging
My cheeks, my eyes screeching to stay alive.

I want to live: O God, to whom I have prayed
Every day of my life – will you never comprehend
That *to live* was my one continual and desperate dream?
Help me a little now; either in, or out, of my death.

Tullynoe: Tête-à-Tête in the Parish Priest's Parlour

'Ah he was a grand man.'
'He was: he fell out of the train going to Sligo.'
'He did: he thought he was going to the lavatory.'
'He did: in fact he stepped out the rear door of the train.'
'He did: God, he must have got an awful fright.'
'He did: he saw that it wasn't the lavatory at all.'
'He did: he saw that it was the railway tracks going away
    from him.'
'He did: I wonder if. . . but he was a grand man.'
'He was: he had the most expensive Toyota you can buy.'
'He had: well it was only beautiful.'
'It was: he used to have an Audi.'
'He had: as a matter of fact he used to have two Audis.'
'He had: and then he had an Avenger.'
'He had: and then he had a Volvo.'
'He had: in the beginning he had a lot of Volkses.'
'He had: he was a great man for the Volkses.'
'He was: did he once have an Escort?'
'He had not: he had a son a doctor.'
'He had: and he had a Morris Minor too.'
'He had: he had a sister a hairdresser in Kilmallock.'
'He had: he had another sister a hairdresser in Ballybunion.'
'He had: he was put in a coffin which was put in his father's cart.'
'He was: his lady wife sat on top of the coffin driving the donkey.'
'She did: Ah but he was a grand man.'
'He was: he was a grand man. . .'
'Good night, Father.'
'Good night, Mary.'

Charlie's Mother

Brendan, does *your* mother have a hold over *you*?
Mine does over *me*. I keep beseeching her
To take her purple-veined hand out of my head
But do you know what she says, the old cabbage?
Stirring and churning her hand round inside in my head
She crows: 'Charlie m'boy, you've got a lot of neck.'

Mind you, when I think about it, she has a point:
My neck *is* thick and there *is* rather a lot of it;
And look at all the *mun* I have made
Without having to do a flick of work for it.
I rub my neck wryly when Mother crows:
'That's m'boy, Charlie, lots of *mun* for *mum*.'

And you know, Brendan – would you like another drink?
Double brandy there, please – I often think, Brendan,
When I look at myself in the mirror each morning –
And I must admit that that's my favourite moment of each day –
Even on black bloody days like today – I always see
Somewhere behind my fat neck my tiny little mother winking
    up at me.

Another drink? Certainly Brendan. Double brandy there, please.
Down, Bismarck, down. Down, Bismarck, down.
Damned Alsatian bitch but a friendly bitch at heart;
Mother gave her to me as a Christian – I mean Christmas
    – present.
Another drink? Certainly Brendan, quadruple brandy
    there, please.
Down, Bismarck, down. Down, Bismarck, down.

But Brendan, you were saying about Micky Finn of
    Castlepollard
That his mother has run away and left him for another man?
Another case, I'm afraid, of not keeping the hand in the till;

20

Not enough neck at all at all. Can you hear me, Brendan?
Come on, *a mhic*, straighten up for Christ's sake – or at least
    for Ireland's sake.
Down, Bismarck, down. Down, Bismarck, down.

Brendan, do you realise, you pixillated, feckless sot,
That if my mother came in here just now, as she might very
    well do
(Mothers tend to eavesdrop in the footsteps of their favourite
    offspring),
She might think that I am to blame for the condition you're in?
You're not just drunk – you're in a coma:
She might even decide to turn Bismarck against me.

Eat him, Bismarck, eat him.
   Eat him, Bismarck, eat him.

Nyum: nyum, nyum, nyum, nyum, nyum; Nyum.

Spitting the Pips Out – with the College Lecturer in Philosophy

When I took up my new appointment as college lecturer in
    philosophy
And I was allotted the subject of epistemology,
I arranged for a svelte Swedish girl
To act as a model for my inaugural lecture.
The males in the auditorium chortled
And the females let off titters – titters.

But – sizing up the situation –
I produced a packet of Hamlet cigars
And, having lit up one, I handed it to my model
So that she could relax the more
On the *chaise-longue*, which with great difficulty,
I must say, I had procured from the chaplaincy.

'Epistemology,' I began, 'is the science of knowing!
Do we know, or do we not know, that this young woman
Is reclining beside me on a *chaise-longue*?
And if we know, how do we know?'
I placed my hand on her left breast but before
I could make my point clear, my words were drowned
In such a porridge of pandemonium as I have not anywhere
    else experienced
In all my peregrinations from Ballyferriter to Düsseldorf
    and back.

There was nothing for it but to take drastic action.
Drastic, Philip, drastic.
I snatched up my files and flung them all at the class,
Jarring them into muteness. And I let the muteness
Evolve until all that was audible was her puffing of the cigar –
Puff. . . Puff. . . Puff. . . Puff. . . Puff. . .
And then I trumpeted: 'Write an essay for next week
On whether or not I am right in saying – nay, asseverating –

That this beautiful girl here is all in the mind.'
When the riff-raff dispersed she smiled and whispered to me:
'Let's go back to my horrid little flat and make love in the mind.'

Making love in the mind – making love in the mind:
I am so ugly and she is so kind.
'Pour me out a caress from your teapot,' she sighed.
And I did just that while she poured a hot whiskey down
    my throat.

Ah yes, the intellectual life. There's nothing to beat it.
Nothing to beat it, Philip, nothing to beat it –
Except perhaps my mother
With a couple of eggs and one very long, very memorable,
    wooden spoon.

KK's Lament for GG

'No, I never knew her,' the widower said
As the clay clods fell on the coffin of his wife:
'I met her millions of times
And in all sorts of places – on the stairs
At noon or in the middle of the night:
On weekdays at breakfast, dinner and tea:
And at weekends at home in the glooms of winter
Staring together into the flames of the fire,
Our eyes watery and our lips dry:
And on holidays in a guesthouse high on the cliffs
Of an empty village on the western seaboard,
Where it rained regularly and the sun seldom shone:
She grew stranger and stranger as she grew older and older:
But no, I never knew her,' the widower said.

The Bearded Nun

Doctor Michael Spollen MA, HDIP in ED, PHD,
Is college lecturer in dead poetry:
He disapproves of the living poet.
Ambition circulates in his lizard eyes and his wife
Goads him on by having a baby per year:
But when she takes her summer holidays with her mother
And takes away the dear little horrors with her,
He likes to dress up as a nun before the bedroom mirror:
'What a lovely bearded nun I am,' he sighs
And strokes his goatee beard with a stiletto forefinger
And smiles and pouts, pouts and smiles:
'O Sister Michelle love thyself,' he whispers,
Pressing his lips against his own reflection in the glass.
But then the doorbell of Yeatscliff rings
(Yeatscliff is the name of his forty-nine-thousand-pound semi-d)
And he glides out the parquet floor to the door:
It is a young man to read the gas meter.
A vile young man, thinks Spollen, such absurd long hair.

That night in a city disco the young man regaled his chums:
'A nun with a beard – far out, man, far fucking out.'

The Anatomy of Divorce
by Joe Commonwealth

My Dearest and Most Hateful Deirdre:
I am reading a new book over breakfast.
(Remember how you used loathe to see me
Reading at meal times and you were quite right;
I much preferred reading to listening to *you*,
Especially at that hour of the early afternoon
When I had had but one chilled bottle of lager
To poultice the parched desert of my palate.)
It's an Albatross Special, ninety-five pence,
Called *The Anatomy of Divorce* by Joe Commonwealth:
Do you know something, Deirdre? If you and I
Had read this book before we got our divorce
It would have made absolutely no difference:
Hope things in the haberdashery are going dashingly;
I'm binding away in my bindery, humph-humph:
Wishing you lots & lots of odium: Seán.

My Twenty-Seven Psychiatrists

I keep the twenty-seven psychiatrists whom I own under the bed:
I go to sleep on the couch to the rapturous song of their howling.

En Famille, 1979

Bring me back to the dark school – to the dark school
    of childhood:
To where tiny is tiny, and massive is massive.

Madman

Every child has a madman on their street:
The only trouble about *our* madman is that he's our father.

Maimie

There in the river I saw her body:
Was it Maimie? Who else could it be?

Marriage, Deafness, and the Problem of Erosion

Do you hear me? If you really care about me, you must hear me:
The cliff is getting nearer to the front door every day.

Naked Girl in Boardroom of Financiers, South Mall, Cork

Pinstripe or no pinstripe –
By your backsides ye shall be known.

Honeymoon Postcard

Weather wonderful – cannot go out in daylight.
Very nice spot – no beaches worth talking about.
Our hotel is skyscraper fifth on left of dual carriageway.
Tremendous volcanic scenery – completely barren.
Tons of love – Donna and Con.

This Week the Court Is Sleeping in Loughrea

The perplexed defendants stand upright in the dock
While round about their spiked and barred forecastle,
Like corpses of mutinous sailors strewn about the deck
Of a ghost schooner becalmed in summer heat,
Recline solicitors in suits and barristers in wigs and gowns,
Snoring in their sleeves.
On high, upon the judge's bench,
His Lordship also snores,
Dreaming of the Good Old Days as a Drunken Devil
Dozing in Doneraile.
From a hook in the ceiling the Court Crier hangs,
His eyes dangling out of their sockets.
Below him the Registrar is smoothing the breasts of his
    spectacles.
In the varnished witness box crouches Reverend Father Perjury
With a knife through his back.
Behind him in the dark aisles, like coshed dummies, lurk
Policemen stupefied by *poitín*.
Up in the amphitheatre of the public gallery
An invisible mob are chewing the cud.
An open window lets in the thudding sounds of blows
As, on the green, tinker men brawl,
As they have done so there down the centuries –
The Sweeneys and the Maughans.
Such slender justice as may be said to subsist in Loughrea
Is to be discerned
In the form of a streamlet behind the house-backs of the town,
Which carries water out to the parched fields
Where cleg-ridden cattle wait thirsty in the shadowy lees,
Their domain far away from the sleeping courtroom of
    human battle.
Is it any wonder that there are children who would rather
    be cattle?

Bartle and Lulu: Channel Zero

'Bartle, we cannot have a house without a child.'
'Who says so?'
'The Corpo – the Corpo says so.'
'Well then, we'll have to have a child, won't we?
We can't go on living in this Ballsbridge kip.'

'But I thought you said you never wanted children, Bartle?'
'Right, Lulu, but if you got to have them, you gotta have them.'
'Bartle, I wish you wouldn't put so much hair oil in your hair.'
'Listen to who's talking: look at all them paper hankies on
    the floor.'
'If you don't want children, Bartle, I'd rather not have any.'
'Children, Lulu, are monsters but we have to have them:
No children – no caboodle.'

'But Bartle, you yourself was once a child.'
'I most certainly was *not*, Lulu: I was *never* a child:
Do you savvy, Lulu? Do you savvy?
I was NEVER a child. I was NEVER a child.'

'Oh all right, Bartle, do you want to do it now?'
'Do I want to do what now, Lulu?'
'Do you want to do what you have to do to have a child, Bartle?'

'Okey-doke, Lulu, throw me over a beer and give the Box
    a thump.
We can watch the *Late Late Show* while we're at it.
All a bloke wants is his caboodle, not a bleeding zoo.
Go easy on the love act – I don't require to be knackered.
All this women-caper! All this children-lark!'

Munch

It is bad enough being a Fallen Man
But being a Fallen Woman – why even
God made Himself into Man, not Woman.
For God knew that while it is bad
For Man to fall, it is worse for Woman.

Munch.

If Jesus Christ had been a Woman
He would never have made it to the Cross.
He would have been by Pilate raped
Or by one of the gigolos with the whips,
Raped until dead.

Munch, Munch.

But if God as a Woman had made it to the Cross,
The Divine Plan could not have succeeded.
For not even Adolf or Clovis or Attila or Joe
Could have stood to behold for two thousand years
The slow hysterectomy of the womb of all their being.

Munch, Munch, Munch.
Munch, Munch.
Munch.

Veronica Shee from the Town of Tralee

Here I am on a cross-channel ferry:
I have run away from County Kerry:
I could not stand it another day:
But well I know there will be hell to pay.

Girls in Dublin reading *Roots:*
Girls in London reading *Roots:*
Girls in Paris reading *Roots:*
Eyed by silent herds of weepy brutes.

Outside the town of Tralee in County Kerry
Nobody knows me.
Yet all in Tralee who say they knew me –
They did not – not really.

Girls in Dublin wearing boots:
Girls in London wearing boots:
Girls in Paris wearing boots:
Eyed by silent herds of weepy brutes.

Now in the Métro – O Mother of God – I remember when
Loneliness for another girl through me thundered.
I was only nine
But I may as well have been nine hundred.

Girls in boots with no roots
Eyed by silent herds of weepy brutes:
Girls in boots with no roots
Eyed by silent herds of weepy brutes.

On Seeing Two Bus Conductors Kissing Each Other
   in the Middle of the Street

Electricity zigzags through me into the blue leatherette
And I look around quick and yes –
All faces are in a state of shock:
By Christ – this bus ride
Will be the bus ride to beat all bus rides.

Sure enough the conductor comes waltzing up the stairs –
The winding stairs –
And he comes up the aisle a-hopping and a-whooping.
So I take my chance
Being part of the dance.
I say: 'A penny, please.'
'Certainly, sir,' he replies,
And rummages in his satchel
Until he fishes out a tiny penny,
An eenshy-weenshy penny,
Which he hands me, crooning –
'That's especially for you, sir – thank you, sir.'

So there it is, or was.
Will the day or night ever come when I will see
Two policemen at a street corner caressing each other?
Let the prisoners escape, conceal them in a sunbeam?
O my dear Guard William, O my darling Guard John.

The Boy Who Was Conceived in the Leithreas

My Lord, and Ladies & Gentlemen of the Jury,
I beg leave to opine that you think that you know your man.
– A young middle-class pup who needs teaching a lesson –
However, you do not know that that wild boy
– That ignorant, curly-haired, forked catastrophe
Of a nineteen-year-old boy stooped there in the dock –
Was conceived in the *leithreas*
While the Dublin-to-Cork train was stationary at Limerick
    Junction:
Swaying, I grant you, but nevertheless, stationary.

And but barely in time too – for the train leapt
Into motion only seconds after the crucial coupling
And the coaches slid to and fro,
Severing their links, or nearly:
And the Madame collapsed halfway off the lavatory lid,
That ignoble dome of black plastic
On which she was spreadeagled so,
And the Monsieur – as Monsieurs will –
Explored for a space to stare at and he found it
Where the soaped-glass window was slid down a millimetre
    to reveal
A thigh of horse-racing track:
And horses pounded through his cranium
Out the coiled horns of his brain to their doom.

And what hath this wretched nineteen-year-old forked
    misérable done?
Forged a few cheques and dreamt himself a billionaire.
Not a ha'p'orth more.
And now his pater and mater do not even share the same bed,
Never mind the same *leithreas*.

My Lord, and Ladies & Gentlemen of the Jury,
I beg that you show clemency to

The boy who was conceived in the *leithreas*
While the Dublin-to-Cork train was stationary at Limerick
     Junction.
I have done.

A Funk in Obelisk

In a town like Obelisk
It takes neck for a boy to walk out with a girl.
But greater neck no boy hath
Than he who would walk out with Suzie Greene,

Of whom even the dour parish priest dreamed
Wet dreams – such was her orbit.
She was hot, small, and spherical like the sun;
Fire-fanged peripheries.

James Mangan was the last boy in the town
With whom she would walk out
– Or so you would have thought –
As we all did think, including James himself.

Poor James – at nineteen his hill-and-hollow face
Under a clump of hair.
He had known all his days small else
But the wars of family life.

After a football match in which James had dropped
The ball, his father barked:
'You are a funk and you will always be a funk.'
Since childhood James had always been dropping the ball.

Until when one wet, grey, empty summer's afternoon
Outside the high wire-netting round the tennis courts,
He picked up a tennis ball and flung it back over.
Suzie Greene called to him: '*Gracias*, James.'

James? James Mangan of Cliff Road?
Being spoken to by Suzie Greene as though. . .
As though what? She sat down on the sandy grass
Beside him, and they talked away the day.

She called to him again: 'Let's not go home to tea.
Let's go for the longest walk ever by the sea,
Until we can go no further than the sea.'
At summer's end she told him they must not

Meet again. Dropped like a ball
Into a ditch for ever, James walked home
To home that was not home and never had been home:
'You are a funk and you will always be a funk.'

He caught a glance of himself in the cracked mirror
Of his bedroom, all tea-leaf wallpaper and squashed paperbacks.
After tea he walked out to the cliff.
Invoking Suzie Greene, he dropped down out of this world

So quickly, soundlessly,
A turkey feather to its doom.
Three cheers for James Mangan of Cliff Road:
Hip-hip-hurray, hip-hip-hurray, hip-hip-hurray.

For My Lord Tennyson I Shall Lay Down My Life

for Anthony Cronin

Here at the Mont-Saint-Michel of my master,
At the horn of beaches outside Locksley Hall,
On the farthest and coldest shore
In the June day under pain of night,
I keep at my mind to make it say,
Make it say, make it say,
As his assassins make for me,
The pair of them revolving nearer and nearer
(And yet, between breaths, farther and farther),
Make it say:
'For My Lord Tennyson I Shall Lay Down My Life.'

I say that — as nearer and nearer they goose-step:
Vanity: and *Gloom* not far behind.
'For My Lord Tennyson I Shall Lay Down My Life.'

The Death by Heroin of Sid Vicious

There – but for the clutch of luck – go I.

At daybreak – in the arctic fog of a February daybreak –
Shoulder-length helmets in the watchtowers of the
    concentration camp
Caught me out in the intersecting arcs of the swirling
    searchlights.

There were at least a zillion of us caught out there
– Like ladybirds under a boulder –
But under the microscope each of us was unique,

Unique and we broke for cover, crazily breasting
The barbed wire and some of us made it
To the forest edge, but many of us did not

Make it, although their unborn children did –
Such as you whom the camp commandant branded
Sid Vicious of the Sex Pistols. Jesus, break his fall:

There – but for the clutch of luck – go we all.

February 1979

PART
II

The Crucifixion Circus, Good Friday, Paris 1981

At the sixth station there was a soft explosion
And it was not the frantic swish of Veronica's towel
Scouring the face of the gory Christ
Like a pulped prizefighter slumped in his corner.
Perhaps, I thought, it is the man in the porch
With the pistol in his right hand clasped by his left,
Held high above his head pointed into space;
(I had wondered about him on my way in)
It was like the air precipitately being let out of a balloon,
Or the rapid deflation of the bladder of a football.
A tall saffron-faced lady in long grey skirts
– Barely able to stand on account of her age –
Had urinated into her massive black silk drawers
– 'My stage curtains' – as she used call them to her
    great-grandchildren.
The gold urine trickled slowly, as if patiently, across the
    stone flags;
Delineating a map of Europe on the floor as it trickled –
Trickled until it had become a series of migrations
From Smolensk to Paris:
A urine sample for Doctor God to hold up to the light,
Or to be microscopic about
– A clue to the Secret Biology of the Universe –
Or for his wastrel son to muck about in.

Her husband gripped her trembling hand
And with his other hand he adjusted the lilac bonnet on her head
To make her look more pretty.
That he should think of that at a time like this,
That he should treat his wife with the exact same courtesy
As he did when he was a young man courting a princess,
And that she should crawl forth from her bed
To topple like this,
To bear witness in a public church,
To risk all or nearly,

In order to stand by the side of the subversive Christ,
These are things that do not make me laugh;
These are things that make me weep stone tears.
In spite of the living scandal of the warring churches,
On the map of Europe there is a country of the heart.

Fellow catechumens looked down askance at the floor,
Then up at the radiant, tormented faces of the agèd couple.
Why do people of their age and station
Behave like this – they ought to know better –
At the Stations of the Cross and – on of all days – Good Friday?
We had not yet even arrived at Golgotha Hill:
The old pair did not look as if they intended to budge from the pool
In which they stood – out of whose banana-yellow ooze
They flowered and towered like agèd tropical trees,
All wizened and green, all grey and fruity.

The wife kept her eyes fixed on the Cross of Jesus.
Her husband kept his eyes both on her and on the Cross.
Urine or no urine
They were going to bear witness to today's Via Dolorosa
Right out to the end;
If the fellow under the Cross – a dark-skinned young Jew –
Extraordinarily long-haired, even if it is the fashion –
Could himself keep it up to the end. With blood in both eyes
And on his hands and on his feet, he too was in difficulties –
Difficulties with his bodily functions.
Behind the Jew traipsed the priests and the acolytes
In linen albs and lamb's-wool surplices:
Voices whispered from the planets: 'And where are your assets?'

When at the eleventh station they crucified Christ
The old man held high his head with glittering eyes,
Like a man in the stands at a racecourse
Watching a 20-to-1 winner come home,
His wife holding on to the hem of his raincoat,
Not unused to her husband's gambling coups – a loser in society,

44

A winner in life. If at night she had a blackout
And forgot to say her prayers (ever since the War she'd been
    having blackouts)
She could always be sure that he would say them for her.
Such things were unspoken of between them
As now they poked their way
In and out the archipelagos and the peninsulas and the lagoons
    of urine,
The rivulets and the puddles,
Until they found the centre aisle
From which they gazed up at the stalagmite organ in the
    far-off loft
Famed for its harpies carved in oak.
During the Stations of the Cross
A family of Germans had been snapping photographs
    of the organ,
With tripod and flash,
Turning their backs on the ludicrous procession-in-progress.

The old man knew that his wife knew what he knew:
That at the end of the War a German soldier
Had hid in the organ loft
In a nest made for him by the sacristy charwoman.
For three weeks he had got away with it until the parish priest
– An armchair general in the French Resistance –
Had flushed him out. The pair of them –
The young German soldier and the young French charwoman –
Were shot in the back of the head – collaborators –
No Jesus Christ to make it a trio, or was there?
The parish priest murmured over his bread and wine
That such things happen, and have to happen, in war.
Just so, just so – murmured a Communist intellectual,
Blood-red wine seeping out of the stained corners of his mouth,
Le Monde for a napkin on his knee.

By now the Crime of the Urine had been doctrinally detected
And the sacristan followed the trail up the centre aisle,

Up and under the organ loft, round by the holy-water font,
Out onto the steps overlooking the Place de la Concorde.
He thought: the guillotine would not be good enough
For people who urinate in churches.
But he consoled himself with the observation that Bonaparte
Had good taste in Egyptian obelisks – painted penises,
    I should think.

In their crusty old rooms
In the mansards overlooking the Madeleine
The two shaking spouses helped each other to undress.
Having laid their two windowsills
With breadcrumbs for the pigeons,
They climbed into bed into one another's arms,
In an exhaustion beyond even their own contemplation –
Beyond the trees and the water, beyond youth and childhood.
He was the first to fall asleep, his eyelids like forest streams,
And the sun – high in the west over the Eiffel Tower and
    St-Cloud –
Framed his golden white-haired face like a face in a shrine –
A gaunt embryo in a monstrance.
As sleep came over her she heard him say in his sleep:
'To keep one another warm – warm as urine.'
And in Byzantium she saw the gold urine
Mosaicise in her sleep-fog like breath:
A diptych of Madonna and Child – at Birth and at Death.

PART
III

The Man Whose Name Was Shakespeare

I knew a man whose name was Shakespeare.
His first name was William and he wrote plays
For a living. Pretty daring plays they were too.

Yet he himself lived a quiet life with his tempestuous wife:
They used to go to bed early – they were fond of the bed –
And rise with the sun or more often the mist;
He to his desk, his sonnets, and his plays;
His wild, wild humour like wild, wild whiskey.

They invented games and on summer evenings they played
A species of tennis in the back garden, with the river
On one side and the jailhouse on the other:
When they died – they died together in their sleep –
I served a refrain for them which has one double theme:

Play it deep to the backhand, oh Will, will you, my dear,
Or a lob to my smash?
Play it deep to the backhand, oh Will, you will, my dear,
Or a lob to my smash.

The Woman Who Keeps Her Breasts in the Back Garden

Why do you keep your breasts in the back garden?
Well – it's a male-dominated society, isn't it?
Yes, I know it is, but could you explain. . .?
Certainly I'll explain, certainly:
Seeing as how it's a male-dominated society
And there is all this ballyhoo about breasts,
I decided to keep my pair of breasts in the back garden
And once or twice a day I take them out for a walk
– Usually on a leash but sometimes I unleash them –
And they jump up and down and prance a bit
And in that way the males can get their bosom-gaping done with
And I can get on with my other activities.
I used to leave them out at night under the glorious stars
But then little men started coming in over the walls.
I have other things on my mind besides my breasts:
Australia – for example – Australia.
To tell you the truth, I think a great deal about Australia.
Thank you very much for talking to us, Miss Delia Fair.

Watching Michael Cullen's Strawberry Nude with Friend

The stars are black, the night is blue.
Whoever wrote that you are you
Must have been writing with his eyes open.
But as any snowman worth his snow
Will tell you on a North African shore:
'A man cannot write with his eyes open.
Like any other Russian,
My dream is to draw my mother's picture from memory.
You can only write with your eyes closed.'

The stars are black, the night is blue.
You are all that is not you:
The grave-faced girl in black leather jacket
On a lean Dublin street in ice-cold rain
Is stepping out naked under a North African sun.
Such is her fragile nonchalance,
Such is her shy insouciance,
She is the epitome of the vertical swimmer!
Her prehistoric future! Her stereophonic past!

The stars are black, the night is blue.
I must not think that I am you.
I am the eye of the needle through whose strawberry steel
You, who are a strawberry camel, are passing.
When even you're with me, how I miss you!
With what simultaneity you keep your balance
On the Ferris Wheel of Fate! While you laugh at me,
Beneath you far below in the fairground!
A cucumber lonely for his strawberry nude!

The stars are black, the night is blue.
There is a palm tree peering down at you:
A palm tree with an eye in the top of its head.
I am bright with jealousy, bright with it,
Jealous as the night and the moon is a spacefish

Swimming down into the black mouth of your thigh.
O that sky-high palm tree! What a phallic fellow!
What shoulder blades! What hips! Yet a small conifer
Is courting you, cloaked in a parasol!

The stars are black, the night is blue.
What will I do?
Tell the world about strawberry – strawberry you?
But who is your friend with eyes of blue?
It seems to me that you've got a rendezvous
With a snowman in a black djelaba.
I can see the blue eyes in the back of his head
And he is advancing like an empty bed;
No dog is going to get between him and his strawberry nude!

The stars are black, the night is blue.
I don't understand it but of course you do.
A herd of sleeping zebra, one of whom is me,
Dream of being trampled to death by you.
Out in the desert a strawberry woman
Is giving birth to a tiny strawberry man
While she attends the funeral of a big strawberry man;
On either side of her, concertinas of strawberry men
Queue up to give her a strawberry kiss.
Isn't it strawberry, strawberry, that it's all so strawberry!

There *is* a life after language! Bury me.
O my strawberry girl – bury me.

The Rose of Blackpool

He was a goalkeeper and I am a postmistress
And the pair of us believed – I say 'believed' – in Valentine's Day.
What chance had we?
(I speak in hindsight, of course:
I would not have spoken like that in front of the Great Irish Elk
Or, for that matter, in front of a twenty-two-inch colour TV.)
What chance had we?
Every chance – and at the same time not a chance in the world.

You see, I had my own little post office at the very top of the hill
And I kept it completely and absolutely empty except for
    the counter.
One day he had said: 'You are the Rose of Blackpool':
And that night in bed on my own with my head in the pillow
(*Feathers,* I may say – I cannot abide *Foam* –
Nor could *he*)
I whispered to myself: 'All right, that's what I'll be,
I'll be – the Rose of Blackpool.'

Many's the Valentine's Day that went by
Before I got my hands on a PO of my own
But got it I did – and right on top of the hill!
And in that bare, spic and span, unfurnished shop,
With its solitary counter at the very far end,
I stood like a flower in a flowerpot
All the day long – drips & leaves & what-have-ye:
All the year round – '*Number 365, are you still alive?*'
And when the door of my PO opened
(And as the years went by, it opened less and less and less, I can
    tell you that)
The doorbell gave out such a ring – such a peal –
That the customer leapt – stood dead – and I smiled
Until my cheeks were redder than even
    A Portadown Rose in a Sam McCready Dream.

And I had my black hair tied up in a bun
And my teeth — well this is what my goalkeeper used say —
Were whiter than the snow in Greece when he played a
Game there in nineteen hundred and fifty-three.
The trouble with my goalkeeper was that he was too good
    of a goalkeeper:
He simply would not let the ball in — not even when you
    got a penalty against him.
Now it sounds Funny Peculiar — and it is —
(But then so is Valentine's Day
And all who steer by the star)
But to be a successful goalkeeper in this world
You simply have to let the odd ball in.
Benny would *not* — and so one night the inevitable happened.
We were up in Dublin and the game was being played under lights
And he hit his head off the crossbar making a save
And the two uprights fell across him
And the removals were the next night and the burial was the
    day after.

Of course some people say that he's living in Argentina with a
    white woman.
(I'm brown, by the way, and my name is Conchita.)
But *that's* what *they* say — *what* do *they* know?
I stand alone in my little old lofty and lonely PO,
The Rose of Blackpool,
And I do not believe that there was ever another man in the world
Who could court a woman like my goalkeeper courted *me*,
Especially at away matches at nights under lights.
Benny courted Conchita like a fella in a story;
And no matter how many shots he had stopped in the
    foregoing year
He always — oh he always — and he always —
Posted *me* his Valentine.

O Rose of Blackpool, let Mine be always Thine.

The Problem of Fornication on the Blarney Chronicle

Yes – well I think that there is far too much fornication going on
At the *Blarney Chronicle,*
Particularly in the Reporters' Room.
Indeed the situation is as bad among the Sub-Editors;
I mean – it is one thing to have fornication in the Reporters' Room
But it seems to me quite another thing – quite another altogether –
To have fornication going on to the same or even greater extent
Among the Sub-Editors; and that's not the end of it.
At tea break this morning (actually I had coffee myself)
One of the Proof-Readers,
An extremely personable and sycophantic chap called Ermanaric
    Van Dal.
(Yes, it *is* a name to play with, isn't it? – Celtic, I suppose –
Although it is rumoured that he is of Danish extraction
And I should not be surprised if that's the case.)
Well, he told me that among the Proof-Readers
There Is A Whole Lot Of Fornicating Going On;
It sounds much too much like the name of a pop song.
You simply cannot sustain or indeed tolerate fornication on
    that scale
On a newspaper – certainly not on a serious, low-quality
    newspaper
The likes of the *Blarney Chronicle.*
As for the situation in the Typists' Pool, well I mean. . .
The only thing to do is to get hold of the *Oxford English*
    Dictionary
As well as, of course, of one's own sexuality –
By the way, have you seen the report sent in by Field three
    hours ago
On the twenty-eight-year-old Newry man shot dead in the head
    in front of his kiddies?
A Provisional IRA show.
Horse-Face Durcan wants to run a front-page story on this
But I've had to remind Horse-Face that there's no room on
    the *Blarney*

On the front page or any other page for this kind of
   tear-jerker.
It just doesn't jerk anyone's tears any more.
The dead sod was a Protestant and, besides, unemployed –
As I was saying, we must get hold of the *Oxford Dictionary*
And look up the word 'Fornication' and, if necessary,
Send for the Garda Síochána or, at the very least,
Give the Attorney General's office a buzz – you know the sort
   of bilge –
'Problem of Fornication in Blarney Castle!
Fornication: yes: F-O-R-N (forn) I-C-A-T-I-O-N (ication):
No: it's not *pub*lication – it's *forn*ication:
FORNICATION, fuck it.'
Look: I know what. The best thing to do
Is for Gordon to write an Editorial on it.
(After all there has not been an Editorial-writer like Gordon
Since Thomas formulated in the abstract with his wife,
North-west of Anatolia, I think it was.)
'Fornication In The Backyard' – sort of thing.
On the other hand, the female journalists in the union chapel
Are all militantly pro-fornication,
So that if Gordon leans in an anti-fornication direction
There might well be more pants flying about the place than
   ever. . .
Frankly, Frank, I don't know what the shite to do.
Strange bag of tricks – fornication – isn't it?
They put that Newry bugger's brains in an envelope for
   his widow:
At least there is a streak of decency left in the world.

Old Lady, Middle Parish

When the small old lady introduced the small old man to me –
'This is my gunman' –
I found it awkward to keep my composure.
'Your husband?' – I corrected her, for I considered myself
Well versed in the culverts of colloquial confusion.
'No, sir, my gunman,' she smiled a tiny quiet smile.
'We have been married forty-eight years
And he is the best gunman a woman could have ever had.
If I was to live my life over again,
I would marry the very same gunman.'
I peeped at the gentleman
But he only peeped back at me, his eyes wet with merriment,
His toothless mouth like a knotted-up silk handkerchief,
Orange silk with clusters of black stains on it.
I formed the impression that he was hard of hearing
But in any case she chattered on like a lark's party in Mozart.
'He was a faithful gunman all his life
And now we live in a gunman's flat
In North Main Street,
Just enough room for the pair of us,
Just enough to make do
When you add his gunman's pension
To what I scrape myself – I do for Mrs Dunne –
The Mrs Dunne – Number 3 Winston Churchill Villas –
Just opposite the back gates of UCC –
Two and a half hours, Monday, Wednesday and Friday –
Two pounds fifty an hour.
I like it but it is a queer rake of a house – the Dunne house.
Makes you curious, doesn't it? Curious to know like.
Oh I am always glad to get home to my own gunman
And after we have had tea and watched telly
– *Coronation Street* or *Fame* or the *News* –
We climb into bed – we have got a huge double bed –
From the Coal Quay – old black brass.
It is so high that I have to give my gunman a leg up

When he does not feel strong enough to take a run at it.
That is when I am at my sprightliest – at my most serenest –
Then, and when I am at First Mass on Weekdays & Last Mass
    on Sundays –
Then, when I am there all alone in the dark night
In the rooftops of my native city –
The hills of Cork city all around me
And the moonlight leaping in the window
And my gunman tucked in beside me,
The pair of us back to back;
O my dearly beloved gunman,
Once RIC & IRA; shortly to be RIP.
And out there on the rooftops – the future – like a rooster cock
In the wide-awake silence. . . Valentia 1017 millibars rising
    slowly. . .
God bless him beside me – oh & the poor world too –
The Lebanon – the Lebanon that I used think was Heaven –
And Belfast too and Derry and Portrush –
My gunman used irritate me but he also used delight me
And now I am – yes I am – I am rising slowly into sleep:
If only the whole world could learn to sleep:
You never know but we might wake up in the morning
And cotton on to ourselves: cotton on to ourselves:
Lord, will we ever cotton on to ourselves?. . . Bog cotton.'

Michelangelo Road

What? A little old Jewish couple in their seventies
In their little old house on Michelangelo Road.
'Would you like a book? Would you like a cup of tea?
We are children, and unto children we shalt return.'
The old lady does the talking, and the old man does the smiling:
'He has been cogitating a book on the passage of time:
But that naughty old river outside the window
Is proving to be an almost libidinous distraction.
He says that it has the same effect on him as I did
When I was a girl. Whereas for other men
I was stationary, for Benjamin I was moving:
And now he is having an affair with the River Ladle
Darkly curling in the sunlight outside our window
Instead of writing his tome on the passage of time.
But I am not jealous of the river – I do not flap
My ears at it, for I am happy that Benjamin is happy' –
She laughed like a prehistoric rabbit, unperturbed by the
    firing squad.

Our Lady of the Black Tree, Paris 1981

In those years I was a handyman in a boy's boarding school in the centre of Paris. Early one winter morning I was working in my tool shed on the edge of the basketball court, all rain water and sparrows, when I remembered that I had left my power drill in the refectory where I was boarding up a few windows.

I stepped out into the fresh air but as I turned toward the main building (the refectory was on the ground floor) a movement in a tree on the far side of the basketball court caught my eye. Some boys up to some sort of cafuffle, I supposed.

I stopped, stood still, stared. There, halfway up the trunk of a bare black tree, stood a small woman with an infant strapped on to her, hugging her stomach as if to connect its brains with her intestines. Her face was in a state of decomposition and her jelly-like flesh was frozen in a petrified howl, and she was wearing a nun's wimple. With her right arm she was pointing emphatically at something in the distance but her left arm was missing.

Later, in the police station in the Rue Monge, I was shown the face of an ape photographed in a 'state of terror'. 'Yes, it was the same face,' I replied to the police. I wondered (to myself but not to the police) if the 'state of terror' had been induced partly, if not entirely, by the photographer; had the human being with the camera not produced the camera, the ape's face had most likely been in a state of repose.

There was only one other witness – a young woman with short hair and a long oval black face who had been looking out the fourth-floor window of a book repository in the Rue Lhomond, which overlooked the perimeter wall of the school. Apparently she had got into the habit (she worked as a charwoman in the repository) of peeping at me – a detail which touched my male vanity to the quick.

Her testimony was that she had seen 'no woman in no tree'; the police told me that she had made her statement with unusual passion, almost anger. She did not advert to the fact, nor did the police draw her attention to it, that the tree had its back to her, and therefore she could not have seen what I saw, real or unreal, chimera or catastrophe. All she saw – as indeed all she ever saw, it seems, when she peeped her daily morning peep from that window – was me.

In any case, as I was leaving the police station, standing on the steps in the winter morning gale, the police inspector muttered something about a 'dirty drunken bum asleep in the gutter around the corner – curled up like a fucking foetus, if you'll forgive the expression'.

Were any, or all three, of us on the ball? Or are we all ego-trippers or, as a happy-go-lucky coroner once put it, pathological solipsists? There is only one point which is plain. Life is an abortion. Our Lady of the Black Tree – have mercy on us.

The Perfect Nazi Family Is Alive and Well and Prospering in Modern Ireland

after the painting Peasant Family, Kalenberg, 1939
by Adolf Wissel

Billo is the husband and he played county football
For sixteen years and won every medal in the game:
With his crew-cut fair hair and his dimpled blue chin
And his pink rosé cheeks.
There is a photo of him on every sideboard in the county.
He has five children and he hopes to have five more
And, for convenience, he also has a wife –
Maeve Bunn from Sinchy, thirteen miles from Limerick city.
He keeps a Granny in a Geranium Pot on the kitchen windowsill,
An Adoring Granny.
He is a Pioneer and he always wears the Pin;
If he's not wearing a suit he always remembers
To transplant the Pin to his *báinín* sweater.
He does not dream – except when nobody is looking,
Late at night behind the milking parlour
Or in the pig battery with the ultraviolet light bulb
While the wife is stuck into RTE TV –
Dallas or *Quicksilver* or *The Year of the French*:
And he don't like Protestants and he don't like Artists.
Homosexuals –
'Hitler wouldn't be good enough for the likes of them.'
Lesbians – My God,
A woman making love to a woman
Is unimaginable and, therefore, impossible.
He drives a Volkswagen – the People's Car:
Ein Volk, Ein Reich, Ein Führer.
On Sundays he drives the family mad and/or to the seaside
At Ballybunion in the drizzle.
If any brat in the back of the Volks
So much as gasps
For a window to be opened – just two inches, Daddy –

The heroic driver bestows an enormous clout
On the little head of the gasper.
He is a County Councillor – whatever that is.
Mind you, he does own a thousand-seater pub
For which he was refused planning permission
And from which there is no fire escape –
Which presumably is why he has never been seen on the
    premises –
The OK Corral on the side of the Buggery Mountains.
In bed his wife calls him – yummy, yummy, yummy –
But don't ask me what he works at
Because it doesn't matter what Billo works at:
Billo is a darlin' boy and that's all that matters.
All that matters is that Billo is a darlin' boy:
All that matters is that Billo is a darlin' boy:
All that matters is that Billo is a darlin' boy:
HEIL!

Interview for a Job

— I had a nervous breakdown when I was seventeen.
— You had not?
— I had.
— But how could a beautiful girl like you
  Have had such a thing as a nervous breakdown?
— I don't know, sir.
— But you have such luscious hair!
— They said I had some kind of depression.
— With long black curls like yours? Depression?
— Erogenous depression.
— Erogenous depression?
— It's a new kind of depression, sir.
— You're wearing clothes, do you know that?
— Am I?
— You are: I like your lips too.
— My lips?
— Your lips: they're kissable.
— Kissable?
— And your hips: I would say they handle well.
— I beg your pardon, sir?
— Tell me, what kind of man is your father?
— He stays in bed every second week.
— Your mother?
— She stays in bed every second week as well.
— A happy Irish marriage.
— Why do you say that, sir?
— Well, it's not every husband and wife who go to bed together
  For a whole week, every second week.
— You misunderstand, sir; they take it in turns.
— OK: so you want a job?
— Yes, sir.
— Well you can't have one.
— I beg your pardon, sir?
— You had one hell of a nerve applying for a job.
  You have no right to have a job here or anywhere.

Get out of my office before I bellow for my Little Willie
To kick you in the buck teeth and whack you on the bottom.
— Thank you verra much, sir.
— Don't mention it, girrul.
— Well then, sir, d'ye mind if I sit on in your office for five minutes:
It is terrible cold outside and I have no overcoat.
— Bloody woman, shag off; vamoose; make yourself scarce.
— But sir, I *am* scarce; my name on the form. . . *Scarcity*.
— Now *Scarcity*, don't act the smart ass with me: beat it.

The Child on the Train, Yorkshire 1980

There was a child in the carriage:
When the train glided out from Leeds
There were only the two of us in it:
Space for both our minds, and space
To bathe our toecaps in the waters of silence.
She was about seven years old, maybe eight,
Long rusty hair and freckled cheeks;
She peered at me, her pink lips sealed;
I strove to read her eyes but I could not.

After York I could bear it no longer:
'My mother was with me at the start of the journey
But after half an hour she got out.'
'At what station did she get out?'
'She did not get out at a station.'

I did not know what to say:
I said: 'Well then, where did she get out
If not at a station?'
                          'She got out
Between stations — it looked
Like a field to me but the train
Was travelling along at such speed
I'm not sure about it.'

Not being able to think of anything else to say,
I enquired of her what she would like to be.
'Me? What I would most like to be
Is a horse: do you know any trainers?'

The wide-eyed pun knifed through the air.

Trains — always it has to happen on trains:
Why does it always have to happen on trains?
'She did not get out at a station.'
'Do you know any trainers?'

The wide-eyed pun knifed through the air.

66

Rory Carty and Son: High-Class Butchers

Mammy, why does it say over our front door –
Rory Carty and Son: High-Class Butchers?
Well, son, the key phrase on our shop front is 'and Son':
You are a little boy – that's to say, a nicens little boykins
With a nicens little knocker on your own little front door.
In other words, you are not a little girlyboots.
Your Daddy, whom you adore, abhors little girls
And so, by being a butcher, he combines business with pleasure.
He buys the best little girls that money can buy
– From Santa Sabina and Mount Anville and the Holy Faith –
And having slaughtered them in his very own abattoir
(Which used be an aviary when we first got married –
He was bonkers about budgies and canaries and home movies –
Mammy reading *Life* magazine on our honeymoon –
Mammy reading *Time* magazine in our back garden –
Mammy reading *Woman's Own* in the Phoenix Park –
Mammy with an overcoat over her swimsuit),
Having slaughtered them in his very own abattoir,
He hangs the little girls in the freezer for fourteen days
(Just like it's done in the Rockall Hotel in Galway)
Before carving them up into choice cuts for the clients
– Psychiatrists, business consultants, art critics,
Economists, poets, developers, architects.
I pray to Our Lady of Fatima that when you're a big boykins
You will become as high-class a butcher as your bloody daddy:
Butchery is such a secure profession for a nasty wee laddie.

The Night They Put John Lennon Down

The night they put John Lennon down,
    Off came my record dealer's lid:
'A pity the bugger did not die
    Three weeks before he did.'
Oh John, in the era of record crap
    It was always good to hear you;
To hear behind your steel voice,
    Your smile a-breaking through.

My record dealer was sad because
    He was almost out of stock,
And all the money that could be made
    With Christmas on the clock!
In death, in life, you beat them all,
    The dealers you would not woo:
And we glimpse behind your granny specs,
    Your smile a-breaking through.

The night they put John Lennon down,
    The night flew out John Lennon's head:
In light John Lennon to the night said:
    'O what is your name, Poor Night?'
'M'name's Chapman,' twanged the night,
    'An' Chapman's a code name, Mark *you*.'
'Imagine!' – wept John Lennon,
    His smile a-breaking through.

The night they put John Lennon down,
    Pat stepped out with Bríd;
And on General Hackett Esplanade
    To John Lennon they paid heed.
The waters bid the ships be still:
    'I will freeze fridges, I will love *you*,
Like walls like bridges' – Bríd sang to Pat,
    Her smile a-breaking through.

The night they put John Lennon down,
   I heard an old man cry:
'O where is the boy? O where is the boy?'
   And he gave the sky a black eye.
An old woman came out of a house
   And John, she was the image of *you:*
'Old man, the boy is not yet born' –
   Her smile a-breaking through.

The night they put John Lennon down,
   A girl clung to a street corner,
Crooning an old oriental number:
   'O My Accidental One'.
The affrighted river whispered to her:
   'You threw me five pounds, did you?'
She replied – 'Here's ten pounds' change' –
   Her smile a-breaking through.

The night they put John Lennon down,
   I heard a third woman call
That the only truth a leaf knows
   Is that it's going to fall.
Oh John, it was a moving thing
   That a lonely heart like you
Should perceive behind a woman's tears –
   Her smile a-breaking through.

Change, Changer, Change. Fall, Faller, Fall.

Papua, New Guinea

On discovering that his girlfriend had done a bunk to Papua,
   New Guinea,
Micky MacCarthy phoned CIE
And requested permission to prostrate himself on the
   Tralee-to-Dublin line,
So that he could behead himself by means of the afternoon train.
'Certainly – *Ná Caith Tobac,*' replied CIE:
'Certainly – Prostrate Yourself – Do Not Smoke.'

However, as happens with CIE,
The afternoon train was delayed for eight or nine hours
(Only the previous week it had been delayed for two or three days)
And as Night in the Western Hemisphere
Commenced to spread o'er earth with starry and sable mantle
Micky MacCarthy felt rather cold
And in the end, after making trebly sure that nobody was looking
And that his pants were properly buttoned up,
He repaired to Cissy Buckley's pub
At Lemass Cross
Where right now he is filtering his cranium with whiskey
And beginning to see the world, including Papua, New Guinea,
In a slightly different light.

The Harpist

May Moriarty came of well-to-do stock:
Private tutor, boarding school, college of music.
When news percolated home
That she was a harpist with the London Philharmonic
Nobody was surprised, the hat fitted.
She under a great harp in the Royal Albert Hall
For ever, and ever, and ever;
A gilded eternity of dress circles;
In saecula saeculorum. Amen.

But it was not to be.
At the bright age of thirty
May Moriarty came home.
Planting her harp
On the sidewalk of the busiest street,
She stayed put thirty-five years,
For the remainder of her life.
People could not make her out
Although they poked and pried.
It wasn't the drink and it wasn't the nerves
Although it should have been the one
Or the other, or both.
Shame on her, whinnied the gentility,
But they could not bypass her
Without furtively slipping a coin
Into the gaping satin purse which hung
From the bowsprit of her harp.
Few dared look her in the eyes
She looked so arrogant, so windswept,
In her music which she played in all weathers,
January and August, October and April.
She bleached her torso in the minds
Of generations of children:
A great white stranded female whale
Plucking harp strings in a gale.

Vincent Crane – the Enniskerry Brat

He was a man who knew he was a woman
Deprived of even the rights of being a woman;
He would give birth to no children on this earth.

Of all human beings I have known
Vincent Crane was the most distraught;
He knew it, yet he contrived to smile.

Daylight – he would walk out the cliffs,
Boys with pistols creeping behind him,
Girls with knives sauntering towards him.
Yet he would not bother to look behind or before him
But he would peer to either side and rejoice
In the cattle in the sea, in the yachts in the field.
Cruel – that when a woman deserts a man –
He has not even the solace of carrying her child.

Mother's Blues

And I would if I could but I cannot, son,
Follow you down to the river.

I remember the night he was born
Thirty-nine years ago
In a room in a basement in Hatch Street.
When the midwife flourished him
High up in the candlelight,
Brandishing him in a makeshift forceps –
(The War was on – which, come to think of it,
Was not unusual – is there ever a time
When the War is not on?) –
Anyway,
When the midwife produced him
He got all red in the face,
Puce,
And the gynaecologist barked: 'Stick him in ice':
Oh he was a quick-thinking gyny, he was.
You think I am joking – but I am not joking:
They put my baby in an ice pack for fourteen days
And if I had been at his christening
(I was not permitted to attend
Because I was a woman
With a head on me – 'You can only come
If you leave your head at home
And bring two pairs of bosoms with you' –
Bishop Ballsbridge instructed me)
– If I had been at the christening of my son,
I would have had him christened 'Snowfire'.
Wouldn't that have been a pretty name?
Snowfire – Snowfire Connolly.
If you listen to it slowly – Snowfire –
It makes Sapphire sound like Sludge.

MAN FOUND DROWNED IN RIVER SUIR

73

O Son of Woman, where have you gone,
Nocturnal in the sun?
Under the water, under my hand:
So near, so dear, so far away:
And I would if I could but I cannot, son,
Follow you down to the river.

And I would if I could but I cannot, son,
Follow you down to the river.

The Elephant House in Berlin Zoo

I am an old woman too weak to sleep.

I sit in the Elephant House of Berlin Zoo,
Alone with a herd of Uganda elephant:
I sit here much of the day with them.
If I could I would sleep with them
Or at least be their night nurse.
Reverberations of a lifetime.
A stampede of gentleness.

I know what it is like to be caged:
To be a teenager in a bicycle shed;
To be a big girl stranded in a bedroom:
The Afghan loneliness of windows;
The Kabul finality of suicide.

How I crave to stroke their pinned-back ears;
To caress their leatheriness;
To massage their pink parts;
To attend to their trunks.

Closing time
And I put away my King James Bible.
A unicorn-like rhinoceros is unloading gallons of urine,
Gold urine,
Into a trough the size of a double bed
With all the finesse of a heavy rainshower.

I can see also through the glass wall behind me
A couple older than myself
Cuddling on a bench.
Earlier today at the terminus
I saw the sixty-year-old driver of the Number 84 bus
Embracing in the back seat with a lady on his knee.

If I could live my life again
I, who all my days have been a refugee,
Would rather have been a Uganda Elephant
Than a Berlin Woman.

        That's the Girl, Big Ears,
Smile for the camera squads.
Curtsy for the telescopic lens.
Sink down to your knees into the long grey grass.

        I am a blank
On which only Death can put a face.
Am I a – was I ever a – member of the race?
O my darling Mozart:
I close my eyes and I behold you
Washing your piano fingers in gold urine.

PART
IV

Jumping the Train Tracks with Angela

The hotel is walking down the street,
*   Hoping we look the other way:*
We will have nowhere to sleep tonight;
*   Nothing will ever be OK.*

The world was only the world when she was there:
Yet in the railway-station bar
There was nobody more disconsolate there than she;
I observed her big-eared smile in silhouette;
Her voice poised in the short grass of her hair:
In jail I know bright hours when I recall
Jumping the train tracks with Angela.

First Love comes always Last.

In the railway-station bar
She hummed an air I do not know;
The other tables and the people at them
Come back into the frame because she was there;
When she went out, so too did they;
In jail I know bright hours when I recall
Jumping the train tracks with Angela.

First Love comes always Last.

Despite the weather and the danger
She liked to stop and look around her:
We stopped and looked at a loco engine
Shunting backwards into a coach;
Until the coupling was complete,
She kept her arm around my waist;
In jail I know bright hours when I recall
Jumping the train tracks with Angela.

First Love comes always Last.

79

Sunlight scarpered along the platform,
Pursued by hailstones with grey hats;
When Angela asked me for protection
I conceded I am myself a racket;
She laughed away my coy chicanery;
She proclaimed to a goods train that I too was good!
In jail I know bright hours when I recall
Jumping the train tracks with Angela.

First Love comes always Last.

She was so sad she could not keep her balance;
She did not notice that I held her hand;
She could not remember her own name –
She who came first in Ireland in Maths Physics,
She who had never savaged a soul;
Oh in jail I know bright hours when I recall
Jumping the train tracks with Angela.

First Love comes always Last.

Alone I went back into the bar; an old nurse there
Disclosed to me that in Heaven they speak Russian;
But – she added – it's the same in Hell:
I sat at the counter staring at bottles of vodka,
Hearing only Angela's brusque *Goodbye:*
Oh yet in jail I know bright hours when I recall
Jumping the train tracks with Angela.

First Love comes always Last.

The Children of Hiroshima, Dublin 7

I

In Prussia Street she bought a house;
A three-storey house with half a roof;
One night we chanced to meet in O'Connell Street;
I enquired if she required help to put back the roof.

Oh we were acquaintances – we were not lovers;
We stood on the roof and ate our lunch;
After nine months she remarked to me:
'Well now that we have got a roof to stand on –

You might like to have a roof over your head:
Would you care to share the same roof as me?
We are total strangers, know each other well,
To me you are just like dirty old bronze.'

'Is that a smile on your face?' I said to her:
'Yes, I think it is' – she frowned:
The sky of her face was a fire on the sea:
She ran out the back – 'I'm gone to get fags.'

II

As I clambered upstairs I had not much time:
In her bedroom I looked at myself in the window:
I saw the mental hospital behind her garden wall:
A kind of football match was going on.

O Jesus – this house is where I yearn to live:
This is the human being with whom I yearn to live:
O Jesus Gypsy – tell me her fate:
Before she comes back through the back-garden gate.

Am I a criminal, awake in the nightmare,
To break into the life of a stranger in Prussia Street?

Jesus – he looked like a Cuban revolutionary – he smiled:
'What's at stake is her heart and not your head.'

The football match was upside down:
So upside down that it looked perfectly all right:
Then she came in the door smoking a cigarette:
I stammered: 'My name is Joe Cross and I love you.'

She waltzed rapidly past me to the mantelpiece:
Tapped the ash of her cigarette into the wrought-iron grate:
Spun around with a smile on the bridge of her nose:
'My name is Nuala Quinn – who are you, strange boy?'

And she threw her arms around me like a slow
Black breeze around a block of flats;
And as we watched the football match in the mental hospital
We sat together on the edge of her bed:

We neither of us were afraid despite the approaching storm:
We exchanged x-ray photographs of each other's scarred bodies:
We had no choice but to go back scarred into Eden:
First, to learn how to sit together on the edge of her bed.

III

In Prussia Street there is a house
With a goldfish bowl on the window table:
And on the floor, close up to the ceiling,
Two lovers float, dead as dead can be.

Of what they did die – we do not agree:
'Of romantic love' – the politicans lie:
'Of nuclear fallout' – the doctors testify:
'They always kept their windows open' – the neighbours whisper.

In the Holy Faith Convent I stab a girl in the back;
In the Christian Brothers' School I slap a boy in the face;

In Eden a priest puts a gun to the head of a nun;
In Hiroshima the bent trees listen to familiar footsteps.

In Prussia Street there is no blue plaque
On the blue house, love, where we did live:
We were against war: we were for blue:
Hiroshima is not, and never was, new!
                    Hiroshima!

The Last Bus to Ballyfermot

Last night in the Kentucky Grill in O'Connell Street
I asked her to marry me and she turned me down!
But she announced that she liked me and since I was hung up
    on her
I asked: 'Will you live with me?' but again she renounced me!
I took the lid off the teapot
And, to the accompaniment of the harpsichord of her laughter,
I fork-lifted up from the river bed two sodden tea bags.
She sang 'Planxty Ó Riada' and 'Buddy Holly's Lament'.
But what finally put the kybosh on last night was that I missed
The last bus home to Ballyfermot.

A bus stop on the quays of the Liffey at midnight!
What an ideal location for the funeral of a friendship;
For the burial of a crane. Knowing that she was pally
With some brilliant young film makers about town,
I speculated in my paranoia if she had earmarked the location!
That my proposal of marriage was a drink she would not swally
Had not stopped her from saying – 'I will walk you to the bus':
We walked along Bachelor's Walk (I am not making this up)
Until on Ormond Quay she declared: 'I am afraid you have missed
The last bus home to Ballyfermot.'

'What makes you so fructifyingly sure?' – I hissed.
My dander was up and there is no more embarrassing spectacle
Than that of a jilted gander with his dander beak high.
Foaming at the ankles, foam ballooned and oozed out my shoes.
Purple in the ear lobes, the Chubb Alarm in my neck had gone off
And, since it was connected up with every garda station in Dublin,
There was not a patrol car in sight, not a garda on the beat. Ah.
Desolate bus stop! Not a sinner except for a saint of the night
Scavenging the trash cans for carrier bags, he cried out: 'Have
    you missed
The last bus home to Ballyfermot?'

'You will have to stay with me' – I hoped she would say.
Instead she said – 'I will walk you up along the quays.'
Which of course was sweet of her but it made meatballs of me.
With a Life Sentence on my head I was climbing the landings:
Inns Quay; Arran Quay; Ellis Quay; Wolfe Tone Quay.
At Parkgate Street we came to the parting of the ways
And when I asked her to sleep the night with me in the
    Phoenix Park
So that waking in the morning we would be ashes together,
    she replied:
'Life is a bowl of cherries, love. That is why you are
    always missing
The last bus home to Ballyfermot.'

And she flew on one wing up Arbour Hill where there's lashings
    of ashes and cherries;
And she flew on one wing up Arbour Hill where there's lashings
    of ashes and cherries.

Forty-Eight Hours in Bed with Joanna

Driving home through the rain from our seaside hotel,
We did not speak to each other:
After forty-eight hours in bed together
We had grown to like one another.

In one another's arms, we can do no wrong.

Through the graves of Glendalough we drove,
Weeping for what can and cannot be:
For the tragedy of the sun, for the victory of the sea;
For the spectacular loneliness of you and me.

In one another's arms, we can do no wrong.

She works night-shifts in the sugar factory;
I work days in a motorcycle shop,
Servicing Yamahas, yearning to flop
Down once again beside her in the top –

In one another's arms, we can do no wrong.

– On the top floor of the hotel by the sea:
She taught me to swim with her in the deep;
And she gave to me the gift of sleep;
Behind her closed eyes the fish reap –

In one another's arms, we can do no wrong.

– Reap freedom from the baited hooks of the tribe;
From lobsters in black blazers with red crests;
Reap freedom to swim among her breasts;
She swimming the breaststroke in my nests.

In one another's arms, we can do no wrong.

Forty-eight hours in bed with Joanna:
She was a blackberry.
She thought I was Finn – not MacCool but Huckleberry.
But she was a blackberry.

In one another's arms, we can do no wrong.

In one another's tongues, in one another's lips;
In one another's caves, in one another's creation;
In the squalid bar of Ireland's most squalid railway station
The bar girl called for a celebration.

In one another's arms, we can do no wrong.

The bar girl announced us as newlyweds
And she inspected us as if we were flowers.
After being in bed with you for forty-eight hours
I know now who are the Big Powers:

In one another's arms, we can do no wrong.

The Big Powers are not the Nation States:
The Big Powers are you and me
And the ninety-nine per cent who are not free:
With you for forty-eight hours, I was me.

In one another's arms, we can do no wrong.

Inland again, and the Dual Carriageway of Pain:
Such Rain! She smiles out of a downpour of Goodbye;
She is a woman who did not lie;
Her black-and-white face above me when I die:

In one another's arms, we can do no wrong.

World Cup '82

'Just so long as this hotel don't go on fire. . .'
I mumbled as you lay on top of me
In our seventeenth-storey bedroom in Seville:
5.30 a.m. – a new morning already beginning.

Making love in the night in Seville is sweet
But waking up in the morning together is sweeter:
To make sleep with you for the rest of my days:
That is my life's goal now – the cup and the world to me.

We make love with sleeping muscles
We have not used since days of childhood:
In the backs of our arms, in the backs of our legs:
You are my Brazil, and I want you to win.

You permit me to kiss you under each ear
And in the small of your back and on each wrist;
And with your teeth you kiss me on each shoulder
And, smothering my face in the pillow,

Again you recline on me with such spiritual prowess –
Like a feather on a windowsill in a gale.
I whisper: 'What makes Brazil unlike every other team?'
You whisper: 'They are used to the heat, I suppose.'

I want you to beat me twelve goals to nil:
I want you to kick the ball through my net:
I want you to bend me and curl me and chip me:
I want to wear your shirt and you to wear mine.

Making love in the night in Seville is sweet
But waking up in the morning together is sweeter:
To make sleep with you for the rest of my days:
That is my life's goal now – the cup and the world to me.

Brother, Can You Spare a Valium?

Brother, can you spare a Valium
For your unmarried sister?
I get the frighteners when I scream
At my baby in her baby-rocker.

Or a sweet box of affection;
Or a coal bag of laughter;
Or a bottle of Sodium Amytal —
I am worn out by it all.

I'm a friend with no friend —
But don't get me wrong:
I prefer life to death
But the pain is too strong.

I adore the trees in the park
But I'm no nature lover:
It's a boy in the factory —
He won't let me get closer.

I don't want him to marry me;
I don't want him to live with me;
I want him only to sleep with me,
Sleep with me, and drown me.

The factory smoke is halcyon
In the blue city air.
Brother, can you spare a Valium
For a lonely bear?

The gossips are a-huntin'
With a high moral gun;
A trapped she-bear in Cabra
Is their idea of fun.

Brother, can you spare a Valium?
I'm too low to get high;
I don't want to go to heaven,
I don't want to die.

I'm a friend with no friend —
But don't get me wrong:
I prefer life to death
But the pain is too strong.

Dave Loves Macker 14.2.83

When you fall in love, you fall:
Fall into water – deep water.
You know that you are out of your depth
But that that does not matter
Because you know also that you are both drowning.

When Dave fell for Macker, Dave fell:
Fell into a nose dive into her lips and eyes;
The further they kissed the further away swam her face;
Her thighs, like her mind, all in a tangle of seaweed;
Swarmy seaweed, all slippery-gold, hairy-green.

When you fall in love, you fall:
Fall into the dream of a long life livid with love.
When Dave said: 'Do you love me, Macker?'
She laughed and she laughed and she laughed:
'None of that now – you're a good bloke to drown with.'

When you drown in love, you drown:
Drown in a drowning from which there is no rescue;
To which both of you demand to be doomed;
Your bodies not to be exhumed for a hundred years;
Found neck in neck at the bottom of the sea.

When you fall out of love, you fall out:
Fall out into the asphalt of a disused pool
By whose edge in the sunny breeze together you exulted
When it was full and the pair of you mistook
A corporation swimming pool for the Indian Ocean.

When you fall in love, you fall:
Two drowned corpses prowling in a snowed-under graveyard
Where the sunken headstones are slumped spectators in white coats.
You stalk each other with all the enmity of pain:
When you fall in love, you fall.

Blind Young Man, Virginia

Some people, of course, opine that I am a con
But I have been blind since birth, never seen nothing
Except a mess of light – a visual soup
That means no more to me than it would to you.
When the noise of the traffic gets bad I switch up the volume:
I could not do my begging except to the sound of music.
Back at the ranch
When the Mamas and the Papas
(That's what we call them)
Want to punish me,
They confiscate my transistor radio.
I think that if I listen to the music for long enough
Suddenly the woman
– Is it necessary for me to say it, for Christ's sake, is it? –
Of whom I daydream night and day
Will land into the solar plexus of O'Connell Street Bridge
And say something like – 'You look wrecked' –
To which I will reply – 'Do I? That's great' –
And in among the shynesses
(You got shyness trouble too? Good.)
One of us will invite the other to have a cup of coffee
In some nice dive in O'Connell Street.

That is exactly what happened on the first day in June.
She's a fiddler
In the North Dublin City Symphony Orchestra
– Third violin –
And when she brings me out to meet her mother in Howth,
Where they live together in a bungalow overlooking Ireland's Eye,
Her mother naturally is pretty afraid for her daughter
And she is not reassured by all the black coffee I drink
And my talk of cliffs – how I love to go for cliff walks –
(Truth is that I have never been on a cliff in my life.)
If I was Virginia's mother I too would be pretty afraid:
Blind young man, with not a penny to my name –

And if we have children, will the children be blind?
God! Are you really God? Or are you, like Santa Claus,
A confection of the Black Forest – an Imaginary Bear?
If I was Virginia's mother I'd be pretty scared – wouldn't you?
Nearly every day now for the last three months
Me and Virginia have met and sometimes she says to me:
'When you're ready, Ray, come in off the bridge':
And I say to her:
'I've got my eye on Ireland's Eye':
And she says to me:
'Say that again, Ray, say that again';
And I do.
I take off my shades and I close my eyes
And I say it for Virginia, I say it again:
I'm Ray on the bridge, man, I'm Ray on the bridge
And I've got my eye on Ireland's Eye;
I'm Ray on the bridge, man, I'm Ray on the bridge
And I've got my eye on Ireland's Eye.

Trinity College Dublin, 1983

I don't think you know what *cobblestones* are. . .
I think that it is just that you like the sound of the words.
Look, do you see that girl over there in the blue jacket?
The tall girl. . . yes. . . in the red slippers?
With the small bloke in the long black overcoat?
Do you know that in her life – she's about twenty-seven –
She has made love about nine hundred times?
Whereas he to whom she is talking
– He's about forty-three –
He has made love about five – maybe ten – times.
The reason that he is lying flat on his back on the ground
And that she is standing with one foot on his forehead
Is that he's nuts about her and she's not altogether quite sane
    about him.
That's what *cobblestones* are for; that's what *cobblestones* are.

The Lion Tamer

'Well, what do you work at?' she said to me after about
    six months
Of what a mutual journalist friend was pleased to call our
    'relationship'.
'I'm a lion tamer,' I replied, as off-handedly as possible,
Hoping she'd say: 'Are you really?'
Instead she said: 'I don't believe you.'
So I jumped up from my chair and I strode across the room
(Stumbling over a wickerwork magazine rack),
I knelt on one knee at her feet and gazed up at her:
Slowly she edged away from me and backed out the door
And glancing out the window I saw her bounding down the road,
Her fair hair gleaming in the wind, her crimson voice growling.
I kicked over a stool and threw my whip on the floor.
What I had hoped for from her was a thorough mauling.
But she preferred artistic types. She had no appetite for
    lion tamers.

The Golden Girl

Yes, I knew her once – the Golden Girl –
Strange name – she dressed always in black –
Guiding a camel through St Stephen's Green –
Teaching ballet to a farmer in Parnell Square –
Hunting for bus stops at night in O'Connell Street –
Like the gold lunula hanging on the blackthorn tree,
Which was which? Was it the black tree
That, in the dying sun, was the most golden of all?
She was the black tree – the Golden Girl:
And she was called by that name
Because she was what she was –
She walked always in circles in a straight line.

The Golden Girl – and you could say –
Yes, you could say – she had a heart of gold:
Which was why there was always a Gold Rush
Of Blokes crazily panning the streets for her:
Yet when one of them – I speak of myself –
Came face to face with her
– Gazing down the gravel of her eyes –
Her heart of gold slipped through my fingers
And her deadpan humour left me standing still:
She was called by that name
Because she was what she was –
She walked always in circles in a straight line.

If you should see her photograph in a magazine
Cut it out – and pencil in the date –
And place it tenderly in your most cherished book
– *Tarry Flynn* by Patrick Kavanagh –
But remember that, in spite of her laughing eyes
And her mouth with its puzzled frown,
It bears no resemblance to the actual girl –
To the real Golden Girl
Whom on this earth you will never know:

She was called by that name
Because she was what she was —
She walked always in circles in a straight line.

One day Gauguin — or was it Picasso? —
I forget which — it does not matter —
One of the big boys — all his admirers
Round him in the art gallery on whose dirty floor
The Golden Girl knelt with a portfolio of her drawings:
What was evident was not that she was beautiful,
Which she was, but that her drawings — unnoticed —
Were more subtle, more muscular,
Than the works of the big boys, and her eyes were tears.
She was called by that name
Because she was what she was —
She walked always in circles in a straight line.

Today it is time to paint the gate —
The gate that will not lock.
Today it is time to speak of love —
Love swinging in the wind.
The State has disappeared but she has remained,
And there are no newspapers — only her eyes;
And behind her the sea — the waiting sea:
The sea waiting to enter the city
Like sleep into the head of a child:
And she was called by that name
Because she was what she was —
She walked always in circles in a straight line.

Going Home to Meet Sylvia

I

I am going down the road with Sylvia;
And I will not be going home;
I am going down the road with Sylvia;
And I will not be going home.

II

I will be going to the Carnival with Sylvia;
I hope to meet nobody there;
I will be going to the Carnival with Sylvia;
I hope to meet nobody there.

III

I am going down the road to meet Sylvia;
Sylvia is not going to meet me;
I will be coming back down the road from Sylvia;
And I will not be going home.

IV

I am going down the road with Sylvia;
And I will not be going home;
I am going down the road with Sylvia;
And I will not be going home.